FINDING YOUR BEAT

AN INSPIRATIONAL GUIDE FOR SPARKING CREATIVITY AROUND THE DRUM SET

CAMERON J BOCK

Published by Fast Hands Drum Studio
Arranged by Cameron J Bock
Edited by Nicholas Schreiber

www.FastHandsDrumStudio.com

ISBN-13: 979-8-9867229-1-7

ABOUT THE STUDIO

Fast Hands Drum Studio was founded by John T. Bock in 1958 in Mt Vernon, NY. After relocation to the village of Elmsford, New York, John grew the drum studio by giving professional instructions to all of his students.

In 1979, John published the first Fast Hands Drum Studio book, "Fast Hands for Drummers in 30 Minutes a Day". The book sold thousands of copies and helped students and professionals develop their drumming techniques.

Fast Hands Drum Studio's mission is to provide the highest quality drumming resources to enable every individual the opportunity to learn the percussive arts.

We continue to give private lessons to aspiring drummers through personalized virtual lessons, printed material, and online resources. We want everyone to realize the beauty, strength, and self-confidence that comes with playing the drums!

DRUM NOTATION

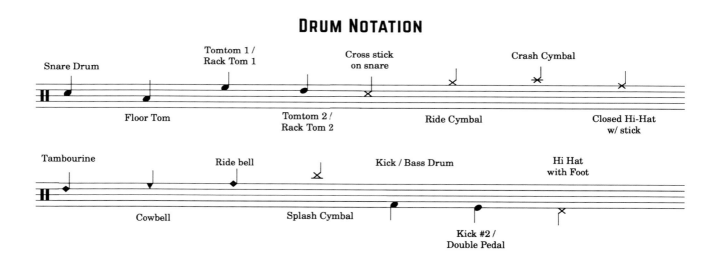

Finding Your Beat is a journal-like manuscript that allows you to harness inspiration from your life and integrate it into your playing. The prompts are formatted similar to a self-reflection diary. Each day, write a solo that takes inspiration from the prompt on that page.

Embracing creativity through these prompts can help drummers to discover unique rhythms and patterns within their playing. By focusing on their feelings and emotions, drummers can tap into their inner musicality and find new ways to express themselves through their drumming.

Trying out different rhythms and patterns can help drummers to discover new ways of expressing themselves through their drums. This may involve breaking out of traditional rhythms and trying out more complex or unconventional patterns. By allowing yourself to be creative and open to new ideas, drummers can find unique rhythms that are truly your own and help to stand out as a drummer.

Chapter One, Inspire, is designed to introduce the concept of thinking creatively behind the drum set. The prompts will add limitations to your playing so that you are forced to step outside of your comfort zone as a drummer. The goal of the limitations is to spark new ways of creating sounds and phrases on your drum set.

Chapter Two, Challenge, is an expansion of the first chapter. The prompts will add tighter restrictions to your playing, further pushing you towards more unique and distinct rhythms This chapter will also begin to introduce abstract concepts into your playing.

Chapter Three, Vision, is written to inject your abstract thoughts and feelings directly into your playing. There are no limitations imposed within this chapter; rather you will set the limits based on the emotions and feelings you choose to communicate.

Commanding Your Rhythmic Coordination is a drum method book designed to help drummers improve their 4-way coordination skills. It features innovative exercises that challenge drummers to play complex phrases and beats they have never attempted before. The book is easy to follow and provides numerous options for developing coordination on the drum set. Get your copy today on Amazon.com and start improving your coordination skills now.

The Professional Percussion Manuscript is the perfect tool for collegiate and professional percussionists and drummers. With its hardcover design and percussion clef, it's sure to make a statement on your bookshelf. This blank manuscript is perfect for taking notes, charting out compositions, or simply organizing your ideas. It also makes a great gift for any drumming enthusiast. Get your copy today and elevate your percussion practice.

Mastering Your Drumstick's Bounce is a drum method book that maximizes the benefits of practice time for drummers. It introduces innovative, previously unseen exercises that help drummers develop greater control and speed with their drumsticks. This book is a valuable resource for any drummer looking to take their skills to the next level. Order your copy today on Amazon.com and start mastering your drumstick bounce.

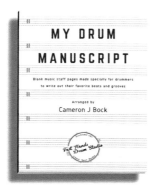

My Drum Manuscript is the ultimate tool for drummers who want to record and save their favorite beats. With its unique percussion clef and guide to each drum on the staff, this blank manuscript is specifically designed to meet the needs of drummers. Whether you're just starting out or an experienced player, My Drum Manuscript is an essential addition to your drumming toolkit.

CHAPTER 1

INSPIRE

To get the most out of this book, aim to practice one page per day. Each prompt will present specific limitations on various aspects of your solo, challenging you to come up with creative musical solutions. Unless the prompt specifies otherwise, feel free to use rests and experiment with different time signatures, dynamics, and tempos to find your own unique voice on the drum set. Remember, the goal is to stretch your musical abilities and think outside the box.

TIP

Think critically about the resources that are available when completing the prompts.

EXAMPLE

If the prompt is "**Solo only on the Snare using Quarter and Eighth Notes**", think of as many unique and different ways you can play quarter notes and eighth notes on the snare drum.

Think about how to use:

ACCENTS	RESTS
RIMSHOTS	TEMPO
TURNING THE SNARES ON/OFF	DYNAMICS (LOUD VS QUIET)
TIME SIGNATURES (4/4, 3/4, 6/8)	PLAYING THE RIMS OF THE DRUMS

Things to think about: Turning the snares on and off; Dynamics; Accents; Playing on the rim of the drum; Time signature; Rimshots; Rests!

DATE:_____

www.FastHandsDrumStudio.com

Things to think about: How tightly you are closing your hi-hats; the bell of the hi-hat; the bottom cymbal of the hi-hat; the hi-hat stand; the rim of Tom-tom 1; remember to add rests!

DATE: _____

Things to think about: Where can your Left Hand reach? How strong are you with alternating between your Left Hand and Right Foot?

DATE: _____

Things to think about: The only limitation is the gradual crescendo from the beginning to the end. Therefore, what drum/cymbal is the easiest to play quietly? How intricately can you play quietly? As you get louder, are you going to change the time signature or tempo?

DATE: _____

Things to think about: When playing the Snare Drum, you may only play two eighth notes, so this means there is no limit on how many "2 eighth note" phrases you may play; Is there a way to make the "2 eighth note" phrases more exciting by adjusting the dynamics or by using accents?

DATE: _____

Things to think about: Playing two Toms at the same time; differences between 2/4 and 4/4; have you used any triplets in your solos yet? Remember to add rests!

DATE: _____

Things to think about: Will you alternate the Right Hand and Left Hand as you solo? Will you play using 2- 3- or 4- way coordination so your Left Hand plays in sync with your other limbs? Will you try to integrate your Left Foot into the solo when your Left Hand is not playing?

DATE:_____

Things to think about: Dynamics; Accents; Remember to add rests!

DATE:_____

Things to think about: The limitation in this prompt is that you may not use any rests whatsoever, and therefore you will be playing without any breaks from the beginning to the end. Think of ways to create excitement, clarity, and variety with only sixteenth notes.

DATE:_____

Things to think about: Use quarter, eighth, and sixteenth notes; Write out the complete solo, and then re-place one note per measure with a rest of equal value; Use crescendos and decrescendos

DATE:_____

Things to think about: The different ways to strike a cymbal; How loud the cymbals will get; How you will use dynamics with your bass drum

DATE:_____

CHAPTER 2
CHALLENGE

Chapter Two, Challenge, is an expansion of the first chapter. The prompts will add more restrictions to your playing, further pushing you to think creatively to create new rhythms and solos.

Playing with specific restrictions can be a great way for drummers to push themselves out of their comfort zone and discover new and creative ways of playing. For example, requiring drummers to play specific drums on specific beats or in odd time signatures can force them to think abstractly and find new ways to approach their drumming.

One way to approach this type of restriction is to focus on the phrase or emotion you want to communicate through your drumming. For example, if you are trying to convey a sense of urgency or intensity, you might focus on using fast and powerful rhythms, or perhaps incorporating elements of improvisation to add an element of surprise.

On the other hand, if you are trying to convey a sense of calm or relaxation, you might use softer, more mellow rhythms and play with a relaxed and steady tempo. By thinking abstractly about the emotion or phrase you want to convey, you can find new and creative ways to approach your drumming.

Playing with these restrictions can be a great way for drummers to challenge themselves and find new and creative ways of playing. Whether focusing on specific drums, time signatures, or patterns, these restrictions can help drummers to think abstractly and find new ways to express themselves through their playing. By embracing these challenges, drummers can discover new and unique approaches to their drumming and take their skills to the next level.

There will not be any tips in chapters 2 and 3. Part of your evolution on the drum set will be to create new "tips" for yourself. Chances are, you are so good that I have not even thought of the tips you are going to come up with.

DATE: _____

My own tips:

DATE: _____

My own tips:

DATE: _____

PROMPT: SOLO WITH QUARTER NOTES ON THE FLOOR TOM FROM BEGINNING TO END, AND USE THE LEFT HAND TO FILL THE GAPS WITH EIGHTH NOTE TRIPLETS

My own tips:

DATE: ____________

My own tips:

DATE:_____

My own tips:

DATE: _____

My own tips:

DATE: _____

My own tips:

DATE:_____

My own tips:

DATE:_____

My own tips:

DATE: _____

CHAPTER 3
VISION

Using these prompts to inspire drum solos can be a powerful way for drummers to tap into their emotions and create unique and expressive drumming. If the prompt is to focus on the emotion of anger, the drummer can use this as a starting point to create a solo that conveys this emotion through their playing. This might involve using fast and aggressive rhythms, powerful dynamics, and perhaps even incorporating elements of improvisation to fully capture the feeling of anger.

Alternatively, if the prompt is to focus on the emotion of joy, the drummer can use this as an opportunity to create a more upbeat and energetic solo. This might involve using happy, bouncy rhythms and incorporating elements of playfulness and fun into the solo. By focusing on a specific emotion, drummers can use their drumming as a way to express and convey these feelings in a powerful and authentic way.

Use the prompts in the third chapter to tap into your emotions, and use the previous prompts to find new rhythms to communicate those emotions.

DATE: _____

DATE:_____

DATE: _____

DATE: _____

DATE:_____

DATE:_____

DATE: _____

DATE:_____

DATE: _____

DATE:_____

DATE: _____

Commanding Your Rhythmic Coordination is a drum method book aimed to help drummers develop their 4-way coordination. Through unique exercises, drummers will play never-before seen phrases that teach multitudes of coordination options around the drum set. With easy-to-understand exercises, drummers will practice unique lessons that will teach them to play complex beats and phrases. Get your copy of Commanding Your Rhythmic Coordination today on Amazon.com.

The Professional Percussion Manuscript is a blank manuscript developed specifically for collegiate and professional percussionists and drummers. This hardcover book is complete with a percussion clef. The Professional Percussion Manuscript will look sharp on your bookshelf. It's also a great gift for your favorite drummer (tell this to anyone who wants to give you a nice gift)!

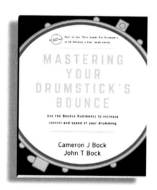

Mastering Your Drumstick's Bounce is a drum method book designed to foster the greatest benefit from the drummer's practice time. Through unique, never-seen exercises, drummers will practice new techniques that will allow them to harness a greater control and speed of their drumsticks. Order your copy today on Amazon.com.

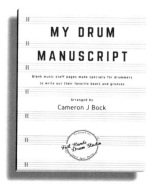

My Drum Manuscript is a blank manuscript created specifically for drummers. Complete with a percussion clef (instead of a treble clef) and a guide for each drum on the drum staff, this is the best book for drummers interesting in writing and saving their favorite drum beats.

Made in United States
North Haven, CT
24 September 2023

41927177R00024